Cryptocurrency

*Comprehensive Insights Into Cryptocurrency Staking:
Selecting The Desired Crypto, Establishing Wallets,
And Detailed Walkthrough Of The Staking Process*

DRAGISA SEEBACHER

TABLE OF CONTENT

All Essential Information Pertaining To Cryptocurrency

Could you please provide a comprehensive definition of the concept of cryptocurrency?

A cryptocurrency (or crypto) refers to a form of digital currency that facilitates online transactions.

You might be curious about the distinctions between this approach and the platforms provided by PayPal or the digital banking application on your smartphone. Superficially, they appear to have the same functions - facilitating payments to acquaintances and conducting transactions on preferred online platforms. However, beneath the surface, their underlying mechanisms exhibit stark dissimilarities.

What sets cryptocurrency apart from alternative forms of digital currency?

Cryptocurrency possesses unique characteristics that set it apart in various aspects. Nevertheless, its primary objective is to function as an electronic payment system under the condition that no single entity exercises control over it.

Decentralization is a fundamental characteristic of a reputable digital currency. It is not possible for a central bank or a collective of users to alter the regulations without first obtaining consensus. The network consists of participants, known as nodes, who utilize software to establish connections with other participants in order to facilitate the exchange of information.

Centralized networks versus decentralized networks.

To the left, you will find the customary equipment utilized by a financial institution. The primary means of user connectivity relies on the central server. Within the right side of the system, a hierarchical structure does not exist as nodes are intricately connected and engage in effective communication amongst themselves.

Cryptocurrency networks possess significant resistance against censorship or shutdown as a result of their decentralized nature. Conversely, a centralized network is susceptible to significant incapacitation through the disruption of its primary server. Determining users' account balances would pose a considerable challenge in the event of a complete data loss and absence of any backup copies in a bank's database.

The nodes store a replicated version of the database within the cryptocurrency network. Each individual functions as their own server. Though individual nodes may experience offline status, their peers retain the capability to access data from alternate nodes.

Consequently, cryptocurrencies are accessible at all times, encompassing every day of the year. They facilitate the seamless exchange of value across global locations, eliminating the need for intermediaries. Hence, they are occasionally recognized as permissionless due to their ability to enable individuals possessing an internet connection to transmit funds.

What is the definition of the term 'cryptocurrency'?

The term "cryptocurrency" is derived from the fusion of the words "cryptography" and "currency," as the foundations of cryptocurrency rest on the extensive utilization of cryptographic methods to safeguard the integrity and security of user transactions.

What is the concept of public-key cryptography and how is it implemented?

Public-key cryptography serves as the fundamental cornerstone of cryptocurrency networks. Individuals rely on it as a means to transmit and receive funds.

In a public-key cryptographic scheme, one possesses both a public key and a private key. A private key constitutes an exceedingly vast numeral inaccessible to prediction by any individual. The magnitude of this number is frequently challenging to grasp.

The probability of successfully predicting the outcome of 256 coin tosses is equally as probable as correctly guessing a private key in the context of Bitcoin. It would be highly improbable to decipher an individual's encryption key using contemporary computational technology prior to the eventual cessation of global thermal energy.

Regardless of the scenario, it is imperative to maintain the confidentiality of your private key, as the title suggests. It is, nonetheless, possible to generate a public key based on this one. The public one may be distributed to individuals without any potential hazards. It is improbable that they will possess the capability to reverse-engineer the public key in order to acquire the private key.

Additionally, it is possible to generate digital signatures by utilizing your private key to sign the data. It bears resemblance to executing a contractual agreement in the physical realm. The primary distinction lies in the fact that the legitimacy can be ascertained by any individual through the act of comparing a signature with the corresponding public key. In this manner, the user is not required to present their private key, yet they retain the ability to substantiate their ownership of it.

The investment of cryptocurrency funds is contingent upon possession of the corresponding private key. When engaging in a purchase, you are effectively indicating to the network your intention to circulate your funds. This is indicated within a message (specifically, a transaction) that has been duly signed and appended to the database of the cryptocurrency (known as the blockchain). In order to construct a digital signature, it is necessary to possess your private key, as has been mentioned prior to this. As an individual possessing privileged access to the database, one can indeed examine the signature, thus ensuring the accuracy and validity of the transaction.

Who is credited with the invention of cryptocurrency?

Several endeavors have been made to establish digital payment systems throughout the years, yet Bitcoin, introduced in 2009, stands as the inaugural cryptocurrency. It was devised by an individual or collective entity operating under the pseudonym Satoshi Nakamoto. The genuine identity of these individuals has remained an enigma up until the present moment.

Bitcoin gave rise to a multitude of novel cryptocurrencies, with certain ventures striving to rival it, while others endeavored to integrate distinctive attributes absent in Bitcoin. Numerous blockchain networks presently possess the capability to facilitate individuals in executing decentralized applications through the utilization of smart contracts, in addition to facilitating the transfer and receipt of funds. Ethereum is arguably the most renowned instance of blockchain technology.

What distinguishes tokens from cryptocurrencies?

At first glance, cryptocurrencies and tokens appear to exhibit commensurate characteristics. Both are capable of being transmitted among blockchain addresses and are traded on cryptocurrency exchanges.

Cryptocurrencies are primarily designed to function as a form of currency, serving various purposes such as facilitating trade, preserving value, or amalgamating both functionalities. Every unit possesses functional fungibility, thereby signifying that the value of one coin is equivalent to that of another.

While initially devised as a means of currency, Bitcoin and other early forms of cryptocurrency, subsequent iterations of blockchain technology sought to extend their capabilities. Ethereum, as an illustration, encompasses more than mere digital currency. Developers will utilize this platform to execute code (smart contracts) on a distributed network and create tokens for various decentralized applications.

Tokens bear resemblances to cryptocurrencies with their ability to serve as versatile mediums of exchange and store of value. You have the option to produce a multitude of replicas or a limited quantity with distinct attributes. They have the potential to encompass a wide range of items, such as electronic transaction records and loyalty points, and they can serve as a representation of ownership in a company.

The primary currency (utilized for transactional purposes or the procurement of services) is distinct from the tokens employed within a protocol possessing smart contract capabilities. In the case of Ethereum, ether (ETH) functions as the indigenous currency that is indispensably required for the creation and transmission of tokens within the Ethereum network. These tokens are created using the specifications of ERC-20 and ERC-721.

Could you please provide an elaboration on the concept of a cryptocurrency wallet?

A cryptocurrency wallet serves as a fundamental repository for safeguarding your private keys. It could potentially be a computer specifically tailored for the purpose (hardware wallet), a personal computer or mobile application, or even a physical document.

The primary method by which individuals engage with a blockchain network is typically through the utilization of digital wallets. Diverse formats may encompass distinct capabilities - for instance, a physical wallet lacks the ability to authenticate transactions or exhibit real-time exchange rates of fiat currency.

Software wallets, such as Trust Wallet, are utilized for everyday transactions owing to their straightforwardness. Hardware wallets reign supreme in terms of security, offering unparalleled protection for private keys against unauthorized access. Cryptocurrency users frequently employ both types of wallets for the purpose of safeguarding their funds.

What is the nature of cryptocurrencies and what mechanisms govern their functionality?

Comprehending the source codes and technical controls that underpin and fortify cryptocurrencies is an inherently arduous task. Conversely, regular individuals possess the ability to comprehend the underlying principles and become well-informed consumers in the realm of cryptocurrencies.

The majority of cryptocurrencies available today are derived from Bitcoin, which was the pioneering digital currency to gain widespread adoption. Cryptocurrencies, akin to traditional currencies, represent value in units - for instance, one could express "I possess 2.5 Bitcoin" in a manner resembling the way in which "I possess $2.50" would be stated.

There exist numerous principles that dictate the significance, safeguarding, and validity of cryptocurrencies.

WALLETS

Individuals engaging in the usage of cryptocurrency possess digital "wallets" housing exclusive data that serves as identification, establishing them as the provisional proprietors of their respective devices. Wallets serve to minimize the likelihood of fraudulent activity for idle units, whereas private keys authenticate the legitimacy of transactions in the realm of cryptocurrencies. Cryptocurrency exchange wallets are highly susceptible to cybersecurity breaches. As an illustration, let us consider the case of Mt. Gox, a Bitcoin exchange which operated in Japan. In previous years, this entity suspended its operations and filed for bankruptcy subsequent to a targeted cyberattack, where hackers methodically looted over $450 million worth of Bitcoin that was being traded on its servers.

Wallets can be securely stored in cloud storage, internal hard drives, or external hard drives. It is strongly advised to have a minimum of one backup, irrespective of the method employed to store a wallet. It is crucial to acknowledge that when a wallet is backed up, it merely replicates the transaction history and current ownership of the wallet, rather than duplicating the individual units of cryptocurrency.

BLOCKCHAIN

The distributed ledger technology, commonly referred to as "

The blockchain, often referred to as the principal ledger, is responsible for documenting and archiving every prior transaction and operation pertaining to a cryptocurrency. It serves the crucial function of verifying ownership of all currency units at any specific moment. A blockchain possesses a limited extent, encompassing a definite count of transactions, which gradually expands to preserve a comprehensive log of a cryptocurrency's complete transactional chronicles until the present moment.

Each node within the software network of the cryptocurrency retains identical replicas of the blockchain. These nodes are part of a decentralized server infrastructure managed by knowledgeable individuals or groups referred to as miners. Their primary task is to continuously record and verify cryptocurrency transactions.

A cryptocurrency transaction remains incomplete until it is appended to the blockchain, a process that occurs rapidly within seconds. The transaction typically remains permanent until it reaches completion. In contrast to traditional payment service providers like PayPal and credit cards, the majority of cryptocurrencies do not possess inherent refund or chargeback capabilities, although certain emerging cryptocurrencies may offer basic refund functionalities.

The units are not accessible to any party for the duration of the transaction's initiation and completion. Alternatively, they are held in a form of custodial account - or, to phrase it differently, a state of temporary suspension. The blockchain system effectively thwarts the occurrence of double-spending, which refers to the act of duplicating cryptocurrency units and distributing them among multiple recipients by tampering with the underlying code of the currency.

PRIVATE KEYS

Each individual who possesses a cryptocurrency is provided with a unique private key, serving the purpose of validating their identity and granting them the ability to engage in unit transactions. Users have the option to generate their own private keys, which consist of integers ranging from 1 to 78 digits in length, or utilize a random number generator. Once individuals possess a cryptographic key, they have the capability to acquire and utilize cryptocurrency. Without the key, the holder's ability to invest or convert their cryptocurrency is rendered null, thereby rendering their holdings inert until the key is retrieved.

While this security feature holds significant importance in mitigating fraud and unauthorized access, it also entails a stringent approach. Disposing of a considerable sum of money by throwing it into a waste incinerator can be metaphorically equated to the act of misplacing or losing your confidential cryptographic key. You have the option to generate a fresh private key and resume the process of amassing cryptocurrency, however, regrettably, the cryptocurrency stored in your former, irretrievable key cannot be recovered. Consequently, astute cryptocurrency users exhibit extreme caution when safeguarding their private keys, securely storing them in diverse digital (typically offline) and analogue (such as paper) mediums.

MINERS

Miners assume the crucial role of maintaining transaction records and serve as objective evaluators of the value of digital currency communities. Miners employ advanced technological methodologies to verify the integrity, coherence, and resilience of currencies' blockchains, leveraging substantial computational capacities predominantly housed within privately-operated server farms managed by mining consortia comprising thousands of participants. The procedure bears resemblance in terms of complexity to the endeavor of discovering novel prime numbers, frequently demanding substantial computational resources.

Miners undertake the task of regularly producing fresh copies of the blockchain, wherein they incorporate recent transactions that have not been authenticated in any preceding blockchain, thereby culminating and finalizing those transactions. A block is the term used to describe any additional element. All subsequent transactions that have taken place following the most recent creation of a fresh instance of the blockchain are contained within blocks.

The term "miners" pertains to the idea that the endeavors of these individuals contribute to the generation of fresh units of cryptocurrency. In actuality, each newly created duplicate of the blockchain entails a dual-component financial compensation: a predetermined quantity of freshly produced ("mined") cryptocurrency units and a fluctuating quantity of pre-existing units acquired through voluntary transaction fees imposed upon purchasers (typically constituting less than 1% of the transaction's total value).

Prominent: Cryptocurrency mining was previously regarded as a financially rewarding secondary enterprise for individuals possessing the necessary funds to allocate towards energy-consuming and hardware-intensive mining endeavors. Individuals with limited financial resources are now unable to acquire high-quality mining machinery that is typically used by professionals. If you are seeking additional income to augment your regular earnings, there exist ample freelance opportunities that offer higher remuneration.

While sellers are not subjected to transaction fees, miners have the ability to prioritize fee-loaded transactions over fee-free transactions during the development of new blockchains, despite the chronological order of the fee-free transactions. This practice serves as an incentive for sellers to impose transaction fees as it expedites their payment process, thereby rendering transaction fees commonplace. While it is indeed technically feasible for a fresh replication of a blockchain to be devoid of any fees, such occurrences are infrequent in practical circumstances.

Cryptocurrencies possess the capability to dynamically adjust the difficulty of creating new blockchain copies based on the level of mining power in operation, as mandated by the instructions embedded within their source codes. As mining power intensifies, the process of generating new copies becomes increasingly demanding, whereas it becomes comparatively more facile with declining mining power. The objective is to uphold a pre-established average duration amidst the generation of new blockchains. An instance illustrating this is the fact that Bitcoin's block time is set at 10 minutes.

Despite the regular creation of new cryptocurrency units through mining, the majority of cryptocurrencies are designed with a limited supply, which serves as a primary assurance of their value. Broadly speaking, this signifies that over time, miners acquire a diminishing number of new units for each subsequent blockchain. Miners are poised to receive solely transaction fees as compensation for their services in due course; however, the practical implementation of this paradigm shift is still pending and may require a significant amount of time. According to analysts, it is projected that the final Bitcoin unit will be successfully mined within the mid-22nd century, should present trends persist.

Cryptocurrencies characterized by a limited supply exhibit a resemblance to precious metals such as gold, in contrast to fiat currencies that possess a theoretically infinite supply.

What Constitutes A Smart Contract Within The Context Of Blockchain Technology?

A smart contract refers to an agreement that is implemented by leveraging blockchain technology. This encompasses a digitalized documentation of all contracts and transactions, meticulously crafted to be accessible to every user within the network. When an individual endeavors to modify or remove a contract, their endeavor will also be recorded in the public registry. This presents a formidable obstacle for any individual seeking to tamper with records or engage in fraudulent activities against fellow members.

Contracts govern a significant portion of our professional and personal affairs, and they are indispensable to the functioning of contemporary society.

The smart contract plays an integral role as a precursor to Blockchain technology, facilitating transactions in a seamless and efficient manner, thus ensuring a high level of coordination. Moreover, moreover, it facilitates various components to prefer applications operating on these platforms to be significantly more accessible. Nevertheless, what exactly is a smart contract?

What Are smart contracts?

smart contracts. PC projects or conventions that are securely stored on a blockchain and operate based on predetermined conditions can be referred to as blockchain-powered systems designed for automated transactions. In conclusion, intelligent contracts. Automate the implementation of arrangements to allow all participants to promptly ascertain the outcome, eliminating the need for a mediator or any delays.

• Smart contracts are contracts that execute themselves, with the terms of the agreement being directly encoded into lines of code within the purchaser-merchant arrangement.

• According to Scratch Szabo, an American computer scientist who developed a digital currency known as "Bit Gold" in 1998, smart contracts. These are automated trading conventions that carry out contractual stipulations.

•Employing it ensures that the transactions become easily identifiable, uncomplicated, and irreversible.

Advantages of smart contracts.

Accuracy, Velocity, and Competence

• The contract is expeditiously executed upon the fulfillment of a condition. • Once a condition is met, the contract is promptly executed. • The contract is swiftly executed once the stipulated condition is satisfied.

• Due to the sophisticated and automated nature of smart contracts, there is no need for any administrative tasks to be undertaken or supervised.

• There was no allocation of time towards rectifying errors that may occur during the manual finalization of documentation.

Trust and Straightforwardness

• There is a significant justification to feel concerned about individual data being tampered with for personal gain, as there are no external parties involved.

• Members engage in the trading of scrambled exchange logs.

Security

•Due to the encryption of blockchain exchange records, their vulnerability to hacking is significantly reduced.

Furthermore, considering that each segment within a distributed document is interconnected with the others, any modifications to a single file would require hackers to alter the entire chain.

Reserve funds

•smart contracts. Eliminate the necessity for mediators to oversee transactions, along with the associated time delays and costs.

What is the operational mechanism of smart contracts?

A smart contract is a form of program that encompasses business logic and operates on a specialized virtual machine integrated within a blockchain or any other decentralized ledger system.

Phase 1: Business entities collaborate with designers to define the criteria for the optimal behavior of the smart contract in response to particular events or circumstances.

Phase 2: Examples of fundamental occurrences include the approval of payment, receipt of shipment, or the reading threshold of a utility meter.

Phase 3: Additional intricate assignments, such as assessing the valuation of a subsidiary financial instrument or executing an insurance payment, could be encoded utilizing more sophisticated logical algorithms.

Stage 4: Subsequently, the designers employ a smart contract synthesis platform to author and validate the logic. Once the application has been composed, it is subsequently transmitted to a separate team for the purpose of conducting a comprehensive security assessment.

Phase 5: Employing an expert in internal controls or a specialized network that specializes in assessing the security of smart contracts could be utilized.

Stage 6: Following the approval, the contract is subsequently transmitted onto a contemporary blockchain or alternative distributed ledger system.

Stage 7: The smart contract is programmed to listen for periodic updates from a "prophet," which functions as a highly secure streaming data source, once it has been deployed.

Stage 8: Upon receiving the essential compilation of events from one or more prophets, the intelligent contract proceeds with execution.

Intelligent Communication Lenses and Aerial Safety Measures

We ought to contemplate a bona fide scenario in which smart contracts are employed. Rachel is currently located at the airport terminal, where her flight has been subject to a delay. AXA, a renowned insurance agency, offers flight defer insurance through the utilization of Ethereum smart policies. In such an instance, Rachel is remunerated by this safeguard. How? The intelligent agreement is linked to the dataset which records the status of the flight. The design of the smart contract takes into consideration the utilization of smart contracts.

The precondition stipulated for the insurance agreement entails a delay of two hours or longer. With regards to the code, the smart contracts retain AXA's funds until the specified condition is fulfilled. The smart contract is presented to the EMV hubs, which utilize a runtime compiler to evaluate and execute the code of the smart contract. All of the nodes within the network must yield a consistent result when running the code. The aforementioned result has been duly documented in the fragmented record. If the flight is delayed beyond a duration of two hours, it follows that the smart contract automatically executes itself, thus ensuring that Rachel is appropriately compensated. Smart contracts are immutable; the terms of the agreement cannot be altered by anyone.

Engaging in voting procedures and Implementing smart contracts using Blockchain technology

Incorporating Blockchain technology within the democratic process can effectively address commonplace challenges. A concentrated democratic framework encounters obstacles in terms of adhering to votes - such as the manipulation of characters, inaccuracies, or biases by election officials. By employing a smart contract, specific provisions are predetermined within the contractual agreement. It is impermissible for any individual to exercise their right to vote through a computerized persona different from their own. The counting is secure. Every ballot is registered within a blockchain network, and the tallying is executed automatically without any intervention from a third party or reliance on a manual procedure. Each identification document is assigned to a singular vote. Clients on the blockchain network itself attain approval. Thus, the democratic process can be implemented either on a public blockchain or on a blockchain solution derived from a decentralized autonomous organization. Therefore, each vote is logged in the official records, and the data is immutable. The aforementioned record can be readily accessed for the purpose of examination and verification.

smart contracts. Granting you the authority to establish a voting system in which you may include or exclude individuals, modify voting regulations, adjust the duration of debate, or modify the principle of majority. One instance of this can be seen when individuals opt for a particular selection within a decentralized autonomous organization.

Rather than a centralized authority making a decision, an internal democratic process within the organization can determine the acceptance or rejection of the proposal.

Implementation of smart contracts and Crowdfunding via Blockchain technology.

Ethereum-based smart contracts. could be employed to create digital tokens for conducting transactions. One could potentially devise a strategy to generate and distribute their own sophisticated currency by creating a tradeable digitalized token. The tokens make use of a conventional coin Programming interface. Due to the presence of Ethereum, there are standardizations of ERC 2.0 protocols, enabling the contract to seamlessly access any wallet for the purpose of exchange. Therefore, you create a marketable token backed by a legitimate form of equity. The stage transforms into a virtual financial institution, dispensing digital currency.

Suppose you are embarking on a venture that necessitates financial backing. However, who would be willing to lend money to someone they are unfamiliar with or lack trust in? smart contracts. Undertake a pivotal role. Ethereum enables the creation of smart contracts that can serve to safeguard a donor's assets until a specified date is reached or a predefined objective is attained. Given the result, the assets shall be entrusted to the contract holders or returned to the clients. The focused crowdfunding framework typically expresses disapproval towards the board frameworks. In order to counteract this, a Decentralized Independent Association (DAO) is employed in the context of fundraising. The intelligent agreements are predetermined within the contractual agreement, and every participant involved in the crowdfunding initiative is allocated a token. Every single commitment is documented and stored within the Blockchain.

Nft Technology

With the progressive decrease in the quantity of prominent detractors of Bitcoin and blockchain technology, the prospects of the cryptocurrency realm appear extremely promising. This sentiment is bolstered by the continuous influx of innovative projects that showcase increasingly audacious and groundbreaking applications of distributed ledger technology. In the year 2021, Non-Fungible Tokens (NFTs) have surfaced as one of the foremost triumphs.

NFTs are crafted in accordance with the ERC-721 token standard formulated by the developers of Ethereum. Certain platforms provide the means for users to execute transactions with ease, preventing them from becoming overwhelmed by the intricacies of the blockchain technology. The sole requirement for generating an NFT is possession of a digital cryptocurrency wallet. Once the file is uploaded onto the IPFS system through these platforms, the establishment of the non-fungible token (NFT) parameters, which are immutable, is carried out.

Following a thorough assessment of variables including the quantity of NFTs to be generated, pricing considerations, and the subsequent allocation of shares for future sales, the production of NFTs is facilitated through the payment of transaction fees within the blockchain network. After the conclusion of the transaction, the NFTs are transferred to the cryptocurrency wallet and documented on the entirety of the blockchain, where the process of creation takes place.

It is anticipated that the level of trust in blockchain technology will increase, as forecasted by Forbes. The implications of this technology are still subject to conjecture. However, given the burgeoning proliferation of existing applications in the market, it is merely a question of time before distributed ledger technology permeates across all sectors.

In 2017, esteemed analyst firm Gartner made a compelling prediction regarding the broad applicability of blockchain technology, likening its pervasiveness to that of "all things digital." It is undeniable that this foresight has materialized within a remarkably short span of three years. In addition, the Trend Insight Report published by the company also divulged the subsequent projection: "

The valuation of a minimum of one pioneering enterprise constructed upon distributed ledger technology is anticipated to amount to $10 billion. A mere 10% of enterprises will achieve significant transformative outcomes through the utilization of blockchain technology. The inclusion of blockchain technology is anticipated to yield a business value increment of approximately $360 billion by the year 2026, expected to further elevate and surpass $3.1 trillion by 2030.

Presented here are a selection of our prognostications pertaining to the cryptographic domain, derived from dynamic blockchain networks that are manifesting genuine, revolutionary reforms across various sectors.

The realization of interconnectivity is imminent.

Undoubtedly, achieving optimal interconnectivity may require a significant amount of time, particularly given the variable nature of interoperability. The IBM blockchain team has disclosed that, currently, approximately 83% of corporate entities are of the belief that the establishment of governance assurance and standards enabling the interoperability and interconnectivity of permissionless and permissioned blockchain networks play a crucial role in influencing their decision to engage in the overarching blockchain network of the industry.

A total of 20% of them hold the conviction that it is indispensable. Hence, there are already numerous initiatives in progress focused on establishing connectivity between on-chain and off-chain networks, as well as enhancing interoperability in response to escalating demand. An illustrative instance of such a project is Polkadot, as previously deliberated.

Verification of the authenticity of the asset

The adoption of non-fungible tokens (NFTs) entails heightened levels of security and authentication for valuable assets. Trust is of utmost importance in the realm of business, and consequently, the implementation of blockchain technology has the potential to enhance trading and commercial activity within volatile markets. Distributed ledger technology (DLT) instills trust in sectors with limited interchangeability, wherein counterfeiting and falsification, such as in the domains of art and collectibles, are prevalent. Per the findings of research firm Havocscope, the annual value of art theft in the United Kingdom exceeds $480 million.

Technological advancements enable consistent identification of the authenticity of a collectible item. Monitor its provenance. Establish an efficient and legally compliant supply chain infrastructure, accompanied by a comprehensive set of documentation governing the management, ownership, and distribution of its components. This bears a striking resemblance to the ongoing surveillance of Bitcoin throughout its trajectory. The technology will document the historical data of non-interchangeable assets based on the way innovators shape the application's intended functions. Additionally, it will incorporate chronological markers for significant occurrences and offer verified information such as auction prices and other relevant details. NFTs play a crucial role in the transnational economy of Web 3.0, unbounded by national borders. This pioneering advancement remains nascent, and in the foreseeable future, it will witness the emergence of the most optimal iterations.

Blockchain-powered Government Systems

As the negative perception surrounding distributed ledger technology gradually diminishes, governments are increasingly inclined to leverage blockchain for the implementation of various processes. This is due to the fact that it provides them with additional liberty to both engage in experimentation and maintain a level of transparency. For example, the government of Dubai is striving to be the inaugural governing body to operate all of its systems on Distributed Ledger Technology (DLT). Additional efforts are being made by various entities to incorporate it within their current frameworks, with further developments anticipated in the times ahead.

Digital Identity

DLT has the potential to offer universally applicable, blockchain-powered, cross-border identity frameworks for global citizens. This suggests that in the coming years, blockchain technology will not only facilitate the digitization of individuals' identities but also provide additional possibilities for the digitization of assets.

Standardization

The advancement of blockchain technology is occurring at a tremendous rate, and it is reasonable to anticipate its eventual standardization. This measure will guarantee that individuals can readily integrate DLT and engage in collective efforts to enhance blockchain technology.

World Trade

It is highly probable that blockchain will emerge as the fundamental technology facilitating global trade in the days to come. This is because it encompasses a comprehensive array of advantageous and indispensable elements that effectively enable commercial dealings between mutually untrusting entities. Thus far, it has resulted in notable enhancements in the domains of supply chain, logistics, as well as financial and remittance sectors. Trade accessibility is facilitated by the inherent properties of the blockchain technology, wherein all actions are inherently immutable and transparent.

Several Blockchain Startups are likely to experience failure. "The Failure of Certain Blockchain Startups is

Anticipated. "There is an expectation that a number of Blockchain Startups will not succeed.

Similar to all emerging technologies, Distributed Ledger Technology (DLT) is unquestionably lacking in maturity when it comes to its implementation. Consequently, there is a possibility that it may fail to meet the anticipated outcomes of investors in due course. Furthermore, instances of premature implementation of blockchain technology will lead to hasty judgments, unsuccessful advancements, and an utter incapability to attain predefined objectives.

The gradual evolution of this sector will necessitate a patient and time-consuming process of transformation. Several years ago, Gartner made a forecast indicating that the majority of conventional businesses would opt to observe the existing applications of the technology rather than actively engage with it.

This phenomenon is currently underway, evident through the investigations conducted by central banks into the development of central bank digital currencies (CBDCs) following their observation of the accomplishments exhibited by different stablecoins, as well as in anticipation of the debut of Facebook's Libra. However, it should be noted that Venezuela has already introduced a national cryptocurrency known as the Petro. Additionally, the issuance of the "Crypto Ruble" has been suggested by Russian President Vladimir Putin, while China is currently in the process of conducting trials for its digital rendition of the Renminbi. It is probable that additional nations will participate in the future.

Factors Contributing to the Future Widespread Acceptance of Cryptocurrency

As per the findings of PricewaterhouseCoopers (PwC), the rate of expansion of the cryptocurrency market will be reliant on the pace of involvement by the participants. The development of legitimacy among individual participants, commonly referred to as "credentialing moments," will also be marked by periods of rapid growth.

According to their perspective, in order for the cryptocurrency market to transition into the subsequent phase of steady growth and widespread recognition, the participation of five essential market entities will hold considerable influence.

Consumers and Merchants

Digital currencies provide consumers with expedited and cost-effective peer-to-peer payment alternatives that surpass those presented by conventional money service establishments. Moreover, it is not required of them to furnish their personal information in order to avail themselves of these services. However, despite the growing acceptance of digital currencies as a mode of payment, consumers may exhibit hesitancy in utilizing them for the purpose of purchasing goods and services due to their inherent unpredictability.

Alternatively, they would opt to engage in a transaction for it. According to a survey conducted by PwC in 2015, it was found that a mere 6% of participants expressed high levels of familiarity with cryptocurrencies, rating themselves as "extremely" or "very" knowledgeable in this area. Nevertheless, there has been a substantial surge in familiarity since 2015, and consumers are already being granted access to groundbreaking offerings and services that they do not currently have access to through conventional payment services.

This will additionally promote acceptance, as consumers encounter the various benefits of cryptocurrencies, such as expedited settlement times, minimal transaction costs, absence of chargeback issues, and numerous other advantages.

Investors

Investors will contribute to the broader adoption and growth of digital currencies, alongside other key stakeholders. Numerous investors demonstrate significant assurance regarding the prospects tied to digital currency and cryptography. The investors' optimism largely stems from the fundamental value inherent in blockchain technology, as previously discussed. Cryptocurrencies have garnered the interest of institutional investors and the financial community on Wall Street, with the more well-established firms successfully drawing their attention.

Tech Developers

We have also observed a rise in the quantity of proficient technology developers who exhibit a keen interest in the field of cryptocurrency mining. Other individuals have opted to direct their efforts towards entrepreneurial endeavors, such as the development of wallet services, exchanges, and alternative forms of digital currency. According to PwC, it is their belief that the cryptocurrency market is currently witnessing the initial influx of skilled professionals who possess the necessary expertise to propel the industry to new heights.

Nevertheless, in order for the market to achieve widespread acceptance, it is imperative that both corporations and consumers perceive digital currency as a user-friendly alternative for conducting their routine transactions. Additionally, it is imperative for the sector to undertake the development of innovative cybersecurity solutions and establish robust protocols.

Regulators

Regarding the treatment, classification, and legal status of cryptocurrency, governments around the world typically display a widespread lack of uniformity. However, it is evident that there is a gradual shift taking place. Certain governmental entities are initiating efforts to establish regulations for cryptocurrencies within their respective nations, all the while endeavoring to identify the most advantageous means by which to harness the underlying potential of this technology. At present, regulatory frameworks are undergoing variable progress across different global regions.

Financial Institutions

Many individuals are accustomed to availing themselves of banking services, as banks have historically functioned as intermediaries between individuals who possess financial resources and those who require them. Nevertheless, the banks' intermediary role has been diminished according to recent trends. The rapid advancement of disintermediation within the banking industry has been evident.

All these characteristics are bound to positively impact consumers and enhance macroeconomic efficiency without any doubt. Given the revolutionary capabilities inherent in cryptocurrencies, individuals gain the ability to seamlessly utilize a streamlined international payment infrastructure at any moment and from any location. One limitation they might encounter pertains exclusively to their technological accessibility, as opposed to factors such as possessing a bank account or favorable credit history. In actuality, the conversation no longer revolves around the endurance of cryptocurrency; instead, the discourse pertains to the progression and maturation of the crypto domain.

Developing One's Own Digital Currencies

An alternative means of generating income through cryptocurrencies entails establishing your own digital currency. Counterparty, an online platform, facilitates the creation of personalized cryptocurrencies via its blockchain infrastructure.

Merely establishing a cryptocurrency does not guarantee the acquisition of wealth. The majority of cryptocurrencies emerge and dissipate without attaining any substantial worth. It is imperative to consider the process by which money acquires value, which is contingent upon the level of demand it garners from individuals. In order for them to make such a demand, they must firmly hold the belief that it carries considerable value. Prior to its extraordinary surge in monetary worth, Bitcoin attained a substantial measure of social capital. There was an increasing demand for it, driven by people's belief in its underlying principle, which subsequently led to the appreciation of its value.

Engaging in the creation of a cryptocurrency solely for recreational purposes, followed by passive expectation for its growth, is likely to yield minimal results, if any. It is possible that both your mother and your closest companion purchase an amount valued at $10, a sum that fails to adequately offset your initial investments.

Alternatively, it is imperative to integrate your cryptocurrency into a software solution that holds compelling value for its users. Please take into consideration the creation of a decentralized application on platforms such as Ethereum, Blockstack, or Lisk. In order to achieve this, it will be necessary for you to conceive a marketable concept. Augur is a decentralized application (dapp) that facilitates the generation of prognostications, thereby enhancing the accuracy of forecasts pertaining to forthcoming occurrences. FirstBlood is a decentralized application (dapp) that facilitates individuals' participation in electronic sports (e-sports) wagering, while effectively addressing the pervasive issue of corruption prevalent within the industry. Alice.si ensures the accountability of charitable organizations by stipulating that they must fulfill specific obligations before the donated funds are disbursed to them. Each of these decentralized applications fulfills a specific requirement, thus engendering a propensity among individuals to utilize them.

Advantages

The foremost benefit that Bitcoin presents is the freedom it offers in terms of payments. The noteworthy attribute of uninterrupted international transactions, unaffected by government regulations, banking hours, public holidays, or similar disruptions, greatly expedites transactions for individuals seeking to make purchases from overseas merchants.

One additional advantage is the ability to independently determine your own fees. Customers have the freedom to determine the amount they wish to pay, or even opt for no payment at all, when engaging in Bitcoin transactions. The sole factor impacted by your fees pertains to the velocity at which the transaction is executed.

The privacy inherent in Bitcoin ensures the safeguarding of both merchants and customers in the realm of Bitcoin transactions. The transactions are final and non-reversible, ensuring that once a customer has paid for a product or service and received it, it is not possible to subsequently reverse the transaction and obtain a refund. Surprisingly, this fraudulent method remains in high demand amongst individuals in possession of both debit and credit cards. Bitcoin employs the blockchain technology, whereby transactions are permanently recorded, rendering them immutable. Additionally, the anonymity feature ensures utmost confidentiality, shielding all confidential data pertaining to both the client and the merchant involved in the transaction. The blockchain permanently retains solely fundamental information pertaining to the transaction.

Disadvantages

Although Bitcoin is undoubtedly a remarkable form of currency, it is important to acknowledge that there are a plethora of disadvantages that come hand in hand with it. These drawbacks exert a certain impact on the worth, efficiency, and efficacy of the chosen utilization of the subject matter.

The primary and most substantial drawback pertains to the level of acceptance. Despite the exponential increase in the number of merchants adopting Bitcoin as a payment method, its status as a mainstream currency still remains relatively limited when compared to conventional forms of tender. This implies that you are hindered from utilizing your Bitcoin in any location, notwithstanding the fact that, theoretically, it would function flawlessly. As this list expands further, the network stands to derive greater advantage from it, thereby fostering a consequent upward trajectory in the value of Bitcoin, given that supply and demand will naturally correspondingly escalate.

One additional factor that undermines Bitcoin as a favorable investment is its innate susceptibility to volatility. Given the current minuscule value compared to its potential and its rapidly fluctuating nature, the utilization of Bitcoin can prove to be exceedingly challenging. One's valuation can fluctuate greatly from one day to the next solely due to the inherent volatility present. This attribute can introduce an element of unpredictability and frustration when attempting to utilize them.

Guidelines and Strategies for Investment

When engaging in investment activities, it is imperative to adhere to a multitude of regulatory guidelines, wherein certain rules carry more significance than others.

One initial aspect to consider is the principle of longevity. In the context of extremely unpredictable markets, adopting a long-term investment strategy enables you to mitigate the impact of short-term volatility. This grants you, as an investor, the opportunity to mitigate risks. In the domain of digital currencies, volatility prevails, presenting opportunities for gains and losses contingent upon the investing style one adopts. It is strongly advisable to consider the future prospects. When making a selection for a prolonged investment, it is imperative to opt for ventures possessing this characteristic; one must thoroughly scrutinize not just the product itself, but also the individuals responsible for its creation. It is imperative that you possess a comprehensive comprehension of your investment and inquire: shall this particular service be in demand or utilized during the forthcoming years? Does this project face any potential competitors that could surpass it effortlessly? Do the developers demonstrate a high level of dedication? There is a significant element of risk involved until you attain a comprehensive understanding of the true nature of your investments.

The second guideline pertains to refraining from investing in ventures whose nature and functioning are not comprehensible to oneself. If you harbor skepticism towards the project, you will inevitably partake in an upheaval of emotions akin to that of a rollercoaster ride. In the realm of cryptocurrencies, significant fluctuations in prices are prevalent. In the event that one possesses a comprehensive understanding of their investment ventures and exhibits unwavering faith in the associated project, the volatility of market prices shall not induce anxiety. Thus, these three factors necessitate your attention in order to ascertain the viability of a project:

• An existing or emerging need for it - In order for a project to hold significance, there must be a discernible market demand. The determination of this is contingent upon the project's demand. The perception of its greatness holds no significance unless it is shared and

acknowledged by others; otherwise, its intrinsic worth remains inconsequential. When initiating your exploration of the cryptocurrency market, it is advisable to direct your attention towards cryptocurrencies that hold positions within the Top 10 Market Capitalization. There exists a multitude of captivating initiatives. Visit, www.coinmarketcap.com.

• Absence of significant competition – The presence of significant competition will impede the potential expansion of the project. There exists a plethora of cryptocurrencies espousing similar principles - this dearth of novelty shall culminate in rivalries wherein contenders shall consume one another.

• Devoted developers – When making any investment, be it in enterprises, cryptocurrencies, or securities, it is crucial to ascertain the individuals

responsible for overseeing operations. Effective leaders will facilitate expedited progress for the company. A prime illustration can be found in the individuals of Elon Musk, renowned for his ventures at Tesla and SpaceX, alongside the notable figure of the late Steve Jobs, who made significant contributions to Apple. In the realm of cryptocurrency, an apt illustration can be found in the prominent figures of Vitalik Buterin, the mastermind behind Ethereum, and Charlie Lee, the driving force behind Litecoin.

The third principle pertains to directing one's attention towards the platform, rather than merely its features. This holds tremendous importance, as a substantial portion of the existing cryptocurrency initiatives lack substantive value and instead emphasize an abundance of features. You may have valid concerns about the definition of a platform. When referring to platform, we are referring to a cryptocurrency that offers diverse services. To put it differently, it serves a purpose beyond functioning as a purely digital currency. Certain cryptocurrencies are specifically designed for niche sectors such as online gambling or the legalization of cannabis.

Presently, a meager number of 20 to 30 cryptocurrency ventures can be deemed as feasible, thereby rendering the multitude of remaining initiatives relatively inapplicable for long-term investment prospects. Cryptocurrencies like Bitcoin or Ethereum, backed by substantial momentum and widespread endorsement, can be regarded as platforms.

When evaluating a digital currency, it is advisable to draw comparisons with prominent cryptocurrency platforms such as Bitcoin or Ethereum. Consider whether the project exhibits favorable comparability. Is the project deemed to be highly established and renowned in terms of its reputation? If such is not the case, then it is likely that it does not represent a prudent choice for a long-term investment.

The extended-term valuations of cryptocurrencies are established by the prospects of the projects. Small-scale projects possess limited growth potential, consequently making them less viable for appreciating in value over an extended period.

10. Alternative coins - additional digital currencies and tokens

In recent times, there has been a significant proliferation of emerging *digital currencies, while simultaneously, the more established ones are progressively unveiling their inherent limitations. This implies that one of the alternative currencies will eventually displace Bitcoin from its prominent position.*

Undoubtedly, Bitcoin has emerged as the prevailing cryptocurrency, serving as a catalyst for the subsequent exponential growth of other digital currencies.

The originators of BTC published an accessible source code for their innovation, enabling subsequent groups to create alternative cryptocurrencies based on it and foster their progression. Alternative digital currencies are commonly referred to as altcoins, with each possessing distinctive characteristics and target objectives. I have provided a few instances as illustrations/examples:

Litecoin emerged as a digital currency conceptualized by Charlie Lee, a former Google employee, in October 2011. It was designed to serve as a progressive adaptation of bitcoin, drawing on the underlying principles of its open-source code.

The upper limit of Litecoin that can be mined is 84 million currently, with over 51.7 million units in circulation at present. The methodology utilized in the extraction of this particular cryptocurrency bears resemblance to that of bitcoin. Nonetheless, the Litecoin blocks that qualify for the award are generated at a rate four times swifter.

Ripple constitutes both a decentralized payment network and a digital currency operating on an open-source platform. It was introduced in the year 2012 with the objective of facilitating swift, secure, and cost-effective (bearing minimal commission charges, which are subsequently eliminated) monetary transactions of any magnitude.

XRP can be likened to bitcoin at its core: this digital currency is founded on mathematical algorithms, exhibits decentralization, and retains a complete record of all transactions within each system wallet.

But there are differences. The conventional method of inhibiting Ripple is not employed, as opposed to the approach taken with bitcoin. It is not viable to restore this currency; all the coins have already been minted. These items can be acquired through exchange offices (points conversion) or via stock exchanges.

XRP enjoys recognition and adoption by numerous major financial institutions. Several venture capital funds have made investments in this particular cryptocurrency.

NEM (XEM) is founded on the concept of a groundbreaking technology; it enables the creation of numerous services with immense potential, ranging from e-commerce platforms to decentralized social networks, and even encompassing sophisticated financial systems that prioritize decentralization and robust security measures.

XEM provides incentives to individuals who contribute to the economy, enabling users to acquire coins effortlessly by engaging in transactions with one another. This growth model possesses inherent significance beyond the realm of extraction activities. This approach *represents a groundbreaking method of overseeing upcoming developments. Additionally, they have intentions to establish an initial cryptocurrency trading platform, which would be the pioneering platform of its kind, resembling a decentralized version of eBay.*

What is a token?
A token serves as an accounting measure employed to symbolize the digital equivalent of a specific asset's balance. The database upholds token accounting utilizing block chain technology, and access to tokens is granted through specialized applications incorporating electronic signature protocols.
What are the different classifications of tokens?
- Equity tokens are a representation of the company's ownership interests.

- Utility tokens - represent inherent value within the operational framework of the digital platform (such as reputation, scores for specific actions, or in-game currency).

- Asset-backed tokens refer to digital representations of obligations tied to tangible goods or services, such as units of weight for carrots or measures of labor rendered by builders.

With what type of token can one be provided?

Only asset-backed tokens can be provided directly. In this particular instance, the token serves as a digitized representation of an actual tangible asset or service. As an illustration, an individual unit of the token can be deemed equivalent to a single square meter of residential area or the entitlement to attend a single screening at a cinema. The entity responsible for ensuring the transformation of the token into a security is the organization itself, which is engaged in the storage of goods or the provision of services.

What is asset tokenization?

Tokenization refers to the procedural conversion of accounting and asset management, wherein every asset assumes a digital tokenized representation. The core concept of tokenization entails generating digital counterparts for tangible assets, enabling efficient and secure handling of said assets. For instance, a proprietor of a bakery establishes an electronic financial record-keeping system whereby he generates digital representations of obligations in exchange for baked goods - tokens. With a reputation that is quite favorable, this proprietor has the ability to engage in pre-sales of rolls by offering tokens through online trading platforms. In this scenario, it is possible for any individual who possesses tokens to visit the bakery and engage in the exchange of one token for a single roll.

What constitutes the principal distinction between a token and a cryptocurrency?

In contrast to cryptocurrencies, tokens can be emitted in a centralized manner (with control vested in a single organization) as well as in a decentralized manner (with control governed by a predetermined algorithm). Transactions can also be processed and approved in a centralized manner, where all servers are under the control of a single entity. The determination of token prices can be influenced not just by the dynamics of supply and demand, but also by supplementary factors such as the correlation with an external asset, conditional emission regulations, or remuneration structures. Furthermore, in contrast to the cryptocurrency, the token lacks its own blockchain.

How to buy tokens?

Tokens can be acquired via online trading platforms (exchanges and trading outlets), or through direct transactions facilitated between the buyer and the seller in person. The process of trading tokens is indistinguishable from the process of trading cryptocurrencies. Furthermore, it is customary for token issuers to incorporate within the web pages of their projects a feature that facilitates the acquisition of tokens using conventional electronic payment methods.

Where should the tokens be stored?

In the realm of transfer and storage, tokens bear resemblance to digital currencies. In order to accomplish this, specialized wallets are employed, facilitating the storage and manipulation of cryptographic keys, along with the generation and authentication of transactions. Generally, these applications constitute an integral component of the tokenization platform's infrastructure.

What advantages does tokenization provide?

- Enhances the efficiency of trade facilitation, as it eliminates the need for physical asset transportation and the registration of property rights documentation.

- Enhances the security of storing and transferring accounting transactions through the utilization of blockchain technology.

- Eliminates the reliance on intermediaries by enabling their involvement to be defined within a smart contract or potentially even excluding them from the chain.

- Enhances the functionality of the infrastructure, expands the platform through the incorporation of supplemental modules (including multi-level authentication, invoicing, regular payments, and card replenishment).

- Enhances usability by seamlessly integrating numerous platform features into the mobile application's user interface.

What are the benefits associated with the obstruction of tokenization in the workflow?

- Implementation of a robust and dependable database structure, guaranteeing the authentication of

data integrity and reliability at each subsequent stage of the system.

- The dispersal of a single vulnerability (where transaction processing and acceptance is carried out by multiple autonomous servers).

- Implementation of a dependable audit (comprehensive examination of the accuracy of all modifications made on the platform by the auditor).

What are the potential hazards and challenges associated with the process of tokenization?

- Hackers have the capability to lose or steal users' personal keys, which is an unpredictable and uninsurable event.

- Preserving privacy in public lockers proves challenging, as transaction verification necessitates accessing the enclosed information.

- Due to the strict limitation on bandwidth, scaling in a decentralized

accounting system poses a challenging endeavor.

To safeguard the capital allocated to altcoins, it is prudent to prioritize long-term investments in cryptocurrencies that demonstrate considerable potential, as well as those exhibiting a consistent positive trend in the marketplace. Typically, these cryptocurrencies boast substantial communities, exhibit considerable liquidity on exchanges, and their developers consistently strive to enhance their functionality.

What Is Cryptocurrency Mining?

Allow me to provide an illustration using bitcoins, the inaugural form of cryptocurrency, in order to facilitate your comprehension.

Bitcoins are not produced in the same manner as conventional currency; rather, they are acquired through a process known as mining within the system. A miner can be defined as an individual who utilizes a computer equipped with a specialized mining program. The term "mining" is employed due to the following rationale:

1. Similar to any other natural resource, there exists a limited quantity of Bitcoins. Therefore, the upper limit for the production of Bitcoins is set at 21 million. Up to the present day, the total number of mined Bitcoins has exceeded 12 million.

2. Similar to traditional mining in the physical world, the extraction of Bitcoins necessitates the allocation of energy investment. The computer of the miner is required to tackle intricate mathematical problems, and upon successfully solving them, new Bitcoins are generated and bestowed upon the miner.

However, miners are not solely engaged in the creation of new Bitcoins. In addition, they utilize their computers for the purposes of validating transactions and mitigating the risks associated with fraudulent activities. An increased number of miners leads to expedited transaction verifications and a reduction in fraudulent activities. Therefore, it is imperative to provide miners with due compensation for their diligent efforts.

The miner receives a nominal compensation for their effort in verifying the transaction. Miners are compensated twice: firstly for validating the transactions and secondly upon successfully generating new Bitcoins. Sounds profitable? Wait a moment, let's not be in a rush.

Satoshi, the individual credited with the creation of Bitcoin, intended for the quantity of Bitcoins produced during mining to remain consistent, regardless of the influx of new miners. Hence, the challenge of mining escalates proportionally with the influx of additional miners into the network.

If, in the year 2009, one was able to successfully extract a total of 200 Bitcoins through mining operations utilizing a personal computer situated within the confines of one's residential premises. In the year 2014, the mining process for a single unit would necessitate an estimated duration of approximately 98 years.

This is the precise reason why ASIC miners were devised. High-performance computing systems specifically engineered for the purpose of Bitcoin mining. However, due to the significant influx of miners in recent years, the act of mining individually remains highly impracticable. In order to address this issue, the concept of mining pools was introduced. Coalition of miners emerged to address the escalating challenges associated with Bitcoin mining. Compensation is allocated to each miner proportionally based on their respective contribution to the work. That is the process by which Bitcoins are created, through the participation of miners.

4.2 The process of coin creation and transaction verification by miners:

Allow us to examine the governing mechanism behind cryptocurrency databases. A digital currency, such as Bitcoin, is comprised of a collection of interconnected participants. Every peer has a record of the complete history of all transactions and thus of the balance of every account.

A transaction comprises a document indicating, "Bob transfers X Bitcoin to Alice," which is duly authenticated through the utilization of Bob's private key. This pertains to fundamental principles of public key cryptography, devoid of any exceptional characteristics. Once a transaction has been signed, it is then disseminated across the network, transmitted from one peer to all other peers. This is basic p2p-technology. There is nothing noteworthy or extraordinary about this, once again.

The information of the transaction becomes rapidly disseminated throughout the entire network. However, confirmation is only granted after a predetermined period of time has elapsed.

Verification is an indispensable concept within the realm of cryptocurrencies. One could argue that cryptocurrencies revolve around the concept of verification.

While a transaction remains unconfirmed, it is in a pending state, rendering it susceptible to forgery. Once a transaction is confirmed, it becomes irrevocable. It has attained an irreversible state, rendering it impervious to forgery, and has become an indelible component of an unalterable ledger documenting historical transactions, famously known as the blockchain.

Transacting activities can only be validated by miners. This task falls within their responsibilities in the context of a cryptocurrency network. They process transactions, verify their authenticity, and propagate them across the network. Once a miner validates a transaction, it becomes imperative for every node to incorporate it into their respective databases. It has been incorporated into the blockchain.

In this position, the miners are remunerated with a digital token representative of cryptocurrency, such as Bitcoins. Considering that the miner's activity holds utmost significance in the cryptocurrency system, it would be prudent for us to pause momentarily and delve further into this aspect.

4.3 What activities are being performed by the miners?

Essentially, anyone has the potential to engage in mining. As a decentralized network lacks the power to assign this responsibility, a cryptocurrency necessitates a mechanism to safeguard against potential exploitation by a single governing faction. Consider a scenario where an individual generates a multitude of counterparts and disseminates falsified transactions. The system would fail instantaneously.

Consequently, Satoshi established the requirement that miners must allocate computational resources to meet the criteria for this undertaking. Indeed, they are required to ascertain a hash, which is a result derived from a cryptographic function, establishing a connection between the newly formed block and its antecedent. This concept is commonly referred to as the Proof-of-Work. Bitcoin utilizes the SHA 256 Hash algorithm as its underlying mechanism.

There is no necessity for you to acquire a comprehensive understanding of the intricacies pertaining to SHA 256. It is of utmost significance for you to comprehend that it has the potential to serve as the foundational element of a cryptologic enigma, over which the miners engage in a competitive endeavor to unravel. Once a solution has been discovered, a miner possesses the ability to construct a block and append it to the blockchain. As a motivating factor, he possesses the entitlement to append a transaction known as a coin base transaction, which grants him a predetermined quantity of Bitcoins. This method represents the singular approach to generate legitimate Bitcoins.

Bitcoins can only be generated through the successful resolution of a cryptographic puzzle by miners. Due to the correlation between the level of complexity of this puzzle and the computational resources expended by miners, there exists a finite limit on the quantity of cryptocurrency tokens that can be generated within a specified timeframe. This constitutes an integral aspect of the consensus mechanism that remains impervious to manipulation by any participant in the network.

Chapter 3
Bitcoin History

Bitcoin was established in 2008 by an individual or group known as "Satoshi Nakamoto," serving as a decentralized digital currency. The true identity of him, or potentially more than one individual, remains undisclosed. During an online discussion board, Nakamoto elucidated the theoretical framework and underlying software, and further addressed inquiries. His primary focus was on coding, however, he occasionally delved into subjects of economics and politics. His ideological position is irrefutable: he espouses a belief in unfettered markets and a firm stance against fiat currency issued by the government. The aforementioned beliefs served as the primary impetus behind his invention. He disappeared without leaving any evidence behind subsequent to the gaining momentum of his innovation in the market.

It was deployed as open-source software and made publicly available in January 2009. Whilst there were prior systems in existence, Bitcoin is commonly acknowledged as the initial form of cryptocurrency. Bitcoin is widely recognized as the inaugural decentralized digital currency in the global financial ecosystem. Hal Finney, an esteemed computer programmer, emerged as one of the earliest proponents, adopters, benefactors, and beneficiaries of the inaugural bitcoin transaction. Finney was the recipient of ten bitcoins from Nakamoto in the initial bitcoin transaction following the download of the bitcoin software on the day of its release. Wei Dai, the creator of b-money which preceded bitcoin, and Nick Szabo, the founder of bit gold, were both ardent proponents in the initial stages.

Nakamoto is credited with the creation of both the currency network administration software and the underlying network itself. All individuals are permitted to scrutinize the fundamental code. The Bitcoin network operates on a decentralized architecture, enabling individual owners to exercise direct control over it (P2P). Bitcoin made its debut in the public domain through a communication exchange focused on cryptography, during which an individual identifying themselves as "Satoshi Nakamoto" announced their involvement in the development of a novel electronic currency system. This person imparted an overview of its characteristics by making reference to a document obtainable on the official Bitcoin website (http://www.bitcoin.org), wherein the details of this system were described.

The objective behind its establishment was to exploit the prevalent apprehension concerning governmental funds that is widely observed among vigilant observers. Nakamoto posited that the reliance of government currency on the trust vested in political elites and their established system is excessive. It undergoes ongoing management. The courses of action that the financial oligarchs may pursue remain uncertain to all individuals at present. The system is not accessible to the general public. It exerts an inflationary impact. It gives rise to periods of economic expansion and contraction. Furthermore, it is rather expensive.

In contrast to the majority of conventional currencies, Bitcoin does not depend on a centralized entity for its operation. Individuals from various backgrounds have the ability to establish price structures and engage in the monitoring and exchanging of goods and services, be it in conventional brick-and-mortar establishments or online platforms. Each of these findings are derived from a database that is accessible to the general public. Cryptography is employed within Nakamoto's program to provide a level of security, specifically by guaranteeing that Bitcoins can solely be expended by their rightful owner and not duplicated for additional transactions.

Bitcoin was among the earliest and undoubtedly the most prosperous implementations of the concept of cryptographic currency. Nakamoto's notable accomplishment lies in the resolution of the issue of double-spending within a decentralized system, a matter that had perturbed both economists and programmers to a considerable extent. Even during the mid-1990s, programmers engaged in discussions regarding the necessity of a digital currency. However, every endeavor proved unsuccessful due to the absence of a mechanism that could effectively hinder the replication of the currency unit and, consequently, prevent fraudulent activities from taking place.

The Internet excels in the art of reproducing documents. On the contrary, copies have a detrimental impact in the realm of finance. Subsequently, inflation and instability ensue, leading to the gradual erosion of the worth of existing currencies. At some juncture, it is imperative for us to achieve a state where the money stock is fully transparent and predictable. Bitcoin was the pioneer in effectively implementing regulations regarding copying. In order to mitigate the risk of fraudulent activities, the network utilizes a distributed timestamp server, as explained by Nakamoto. This server effectively identifies and arranges transactions in a sequential manner, ensuring that no individual can spend a Bitcoin or any fraction of it in multiple instances. Each Bitcoin is possessed by an exclusive proprietor. This prevents any alterations from being made to them.

The entirety of Bitcoin transaction history is retained within the blockchain, which operates as a comprehensive database for all financial activities within the network. This data is stored within a network of nodes, which comprise computers dispersed globally that operate the Bitcoin software and are interconnected via the Internet. Put simply, if you are using Bitcoin, you qualify as a node. Despite the instantaneous delivery of Bitcoins and the ability to track every activity in real-time, the individual transactions are displayed on a screen utilizing Bitcoin software that effectively monitors the clearing process.

Globally, a daily volume ranging from 25 to 50 million Bitcoin transactions is observed. In contrast to established currencies, this amount is relatively small but bears significance. At blockchain.info, it is possible to monitor Bitcoin transactions in real-time. ListentoBitcoin.com is an engaging platform that offers the opportunity to listen to music generated through the analysis of Bitcoin transactions. The program affirms and validates these transactions. The diminished likelihood of falling victim to double-spending increases as the number of confirmations decreases. A transaction is considered technically irreversible once it has obtained at least six confirmations from the network.

In the year 2010, the identification of a security breach in an initial bitcoin client led to the subsequent generation of substantial quantities of bitcoins. When a different sequence prevailed over the flawed chain, the erroneously generated bitcoins were eliminated. In 2013, prominent online platforms commenced the incorporation of bitcoins as an accepted form of payment. A few examples of these are:

WordPress
OkCupid
Atomic Mall
TigerDirect
Overstock.com
Expedia
Newegg
Dell
Microsoft
Electronic Frontier Foundation

In May 2013, the assets of the Mt. Gox exchange were seized by the

Department of Homeland Security. The Silk Road website was closed by the United States Federal Bureau of Investigation (FBI) in the year 2013.

Satoshi Nakamoto

On February 11, 2009, an individual using the alias "Satoshi Nakamoto" posted a communication on the P2Pfoundation website under the title of "Bitcoin open-source implementation of P2P money." Within this message, "Satoshi" disclosed pertinent details including the official website for Bitcoin, the fundamental features of the system, the written document outlining the system's design, and even the specific location to obtain the initial client version enabling participation in the network.

The authorship of Bitcoin, and the individuals behind its creation, has hitherto remained a enigma. In order to ensure the preservation of their confidentiality and ensure the well-being of both themselves and the network, the individual or group responsible for the conception and development of the Bitcoin network elected to utilize the alias "Satoshi Nakamoto."

The only available information regarding "Satoshi Nakamoto" is derived from his P2Pfoundation website profile, which indicates his age to be 38 and his nationality as Japanese (at the time of authoring this text). Nonetheless, it is impossible to ascertain the accuracy of this information. Nonetheless, considering the structural design of Bitcoin, it can be inferred that its inventor(s) would necessitate a considerable understanding of cryptography and advanced mathematical techniques.

Satoshi Nakamoto is the chosen alias of an individual or collective entity responsible for the creation of the bitcoin protocol and the esteemed reference software Bitcoin Core (previously identified as Bitcoin-Qt). Nakamoto expounded on the concept of digital currency, known as bitcoin, in a paper that was disseminated via The Cryptography Mailing List hosted on metzdowd.com in 2008. In 2009, they released the original bitcoin software, thereby establishing the network and introducing the first units of bitcoins, known as a cryptocurrency.

The accurate identification of "Satoshi Nakamoto" has been a subject of extensive speculation. Several individuals have identified Shinichi Mochizuki, a highly esteemed mathematician who specializes in number theory and currently holds a professorship at the University of Kyoto, as a prominent figure in this regard. It has been conjectured by some that individuals associated with illicit markets and unlawful networks are concealing their identities under the pseudonym "Nakamoto."

Throughout the duration leading up to mid-2010, Nakamoto persistently dedicated effort towards the development of the bitcoin program, collaborating with a group of other proficient engineers. During this period, they ceased their participation in the project, relinquishing control of the source code and network key to Gavin Andresen, transferring several associated domains to distinguished individuals within the bitcoin community, and surrendering control of the code repository and network alert key to Gavin Andresen.

In a correspondence directed towards one of Bitcoin's developers in the year 2011, the individual claiming to be "Satoshi Nakamoto" expressed a desire to detach himself from the project, stating an intention to shift focus onto alternative endeavors. Based on the public bitcoin transaction log, it can be observed that Nakamoto possesses approximately one million bitcoins within their accessible wallets. In June of 2015, the amount totaled US$250 million. The true identity of Nakamoto remains undisclosed, giving rise to significant speculation surrounding his persona. The true identity behind "Satoshi Nakamoto" remains uncertain, as it is unclear whether this name represents a genuine individual, an invented pseudonym, or potentially signifies the efforts of a singular person or collective entity.

Top blogs

Indeed, your comprehension is accurate. Leveraging other blogs within your niche for inspiration and to remain informed about your own blog proves to be highly effective. To be candid, this approach occasionally yields superior results when juxtaposed with utilizing social media to keep abreast of news relevant to your blog. The manner in which you employ this technique is exceedingly uncomplicated. The initial step entails ensuring that the blog you are referencing possesses a high level of prestige within your specific area of interest. Additionally, you will endeavor to observe and assess the prevailing tendencies within the blogging community.

For example, if your blog pertains to the topic of health and fitness, I recommend familiarizing yourself with the leading blogs in this particular field and assessing the content they produce. Frequently, they will publish contentious posts on contemporary subjects within that particular field, which will not only enable you to stay abreast of the field, but also provide valuable inspiration for crafting your blog entries. It is advisable to conduct thorough cross-referencing of the information provided in the blog post, as bloggers occasionally have a tendency to distort or manipulate the news. Please ensure that you possess the most precise and reliable information available.

Ultimately, the utilization of current articles or the latest developments from prominent news platforms will prove equally effective. Articles bear resemblance to blog posts, albeit possessing a slightly heightened level of authenticity. Utilize the most current publications that present the latest information or breakthroughs within your specific field of interest in order to enhance your knowledge. The information furnished will generally be reliable and correct. Provided that the website belongs to a prominent news agency. I highly recommend considering the utilization of this platform.

History

Gaining an understanding of the historical background of your specific field can greatly facilitate the generation of fresh and engaging topics. It is imperative that you remain informed about the latest developments in your field through the aforementioned methods. However, if your objective is to achieve a level of mastery in your specific field, it becomes crucial, if not imperative, to possess profound knowledge encompassing every aspect related to your field, including its historical context.

Having a thorough understanding of the historical background pertaining to your particular field will greatly assist you in several aspects concerning the creation of your content, particularly in regard to two specific matters. Primarily, it aids in enhancing your comprehension of contemporary information, and secondarily, it facilitates the generation of novel content. Primarily, acquiring a comprehensive understanding of the historical context within your respective fields will facilitate your ability to discern and interpret current events more effectively. Given that a significant portion of recent news and discoveries possess a certain degree of connection to the preliminary background of a particular field, allow me to provide an illustration using the health and fitness domain. In the health and fitness sector, the majority of news and research undergoes cross-referencing with preexisting data, as we often encounter blog headlines stating that previously established information from four decades ago has proven to be accurate.

If you solely made the choice to acquaint yourself with current news without giving proper consideration to the historical context of the subject matter, it is plausible that you would be uninformed regarding the historical significance of the information in the news, despite its potential historical relevance. Do you comprehend the significance of having comprehensive knowledge, encompassing historical understanding, in facilitating one's overall development? This phenomenon occurs regularly as trends reach their natural conclusion. Rest assured, all previous actions will inevitably resurge in popularity in due course. For example, upon examining the realm of fashion, one would observe that the current trend derives its inspiration or originates from past fashion trends.

I will continue to reiterate this point repeatedly: it is imperative that you acquaint yourself with and acquire a comprehensive understanding of the historical events pertaining to your particular area of expertise. To achieve a distinct blog with compelling content, one must inevitably delve into the annals of its history. Although I understand that history can sometimes be uninteresting, it is crucial to ensure the highest level of quality in the information you provide on your blog if you aspire to expand its audience and attract potential leads. Individuals who possess a sincere inclination towards the specific area in which your blog addresses will possess extensive knowledge and profound understanding of said area. In order to successfully convert these admirable individuals into prospective clientele, it is imperative that you acquire expertise in the niche you currently occupy. If one were to adhere to the guidelines outlined within this literary work, it would not be long before they ascend to the status of an esteemed authority.

I would suggest acquainting yourself with past blog entries and online discussions to gain a deeper understanding of the historical background within your niche. If you so desire, you may also peruse antiquated literary works pertaining to your subject matter. Ensure to allocate sufficient time during the course of the day to investigate the historical background of your specific area of expertise and diligently assimilate a wealth of knowledge.

This chapter aims to provide a comprehensive understanding of the process involved in initiating your own blog, with a particular emphasis on the underlying rationale behind it. Blogging serves as a highly lucrative avenue for generating substantial online income, with potential earnings soaring up to $300 per day. I trust that this chapter has provided you with valuable information, and we look forward to your presence in the subsequent chapter.

Buying With Bitcoin

Utilizing Bitcoin for the acquisition of goods or services might not represent the most optimal utilization of your Bitcoin holdings; nevertheless, it presents an avenue through which you can obtain exclusive items or services exclusively available for purchase with Bitcoin. If you possess Bitcoin, it would be prudent to allocate a portion for the purpose of acquiring diverse goods. Investing presents itself as one of the most straightforward avenues for generating wealth, albeit it is imperative that one also acquaints themselves with the art of procuring enjoyable assets with Bitcoin.

Everyday Purchases

You have the ability to conduct daily transactions using the Bitcoin holdings in your possession. This may encompass a range of activities, such as acquiring a set of phone chargers or procuring toilet paper through an e-commerce platform. Individuals who engage in routine transactions with Bitcoin frequently possess a substantial quantity of the cryptocurrency. It is more logically advantageous for them to utilize Bitcoin as a means of purchasing necessary goods, rather than undergoing the process of converting or liquidating it into cash prior to making these purchases.

In addition to the convenience inherent in not having to sell the Bitcoin, individuals who make purchases using Bitcoin also enjoy cost savings by avoiding the typical seller fees they would typically encounter.

Merchants Embracing this Approach

Prominent e-commerce platforms have begun recognizing Bitcoin as a valid means of transaction for their clientele. In addition to Overstock.com, which has already been mentioned, there exist several other platforms that recognize Bitcoin as a valid means of transaction:

Dish TV is a paid television service that requires a subscription. With the utilization of Bitcoin, you have the capability to settle your bill, procure pay per view programs, as well as enhance the features of your television service. This is the sole television service provider offering this feature.

Expedia, regarded as a prominent platform for travel arrangements and distinctively accommodating to users who make payments in Bitcoin. On the website, you have the ability to make reservations for flights, accommodations, rental vehicles, and even organized sightseeing excursions. Once you have made your selection of preferred travel options, you may proceed to make the payment using Bitcoin.

eGifter – the leading choice for individuals exclusively seeking to utilize Bitcoin for their purchases. At this particular platform, it is possible to procure gift cards valued at an amount exceeding the sum for which they are being purchased, occasionally even at an equal value. Subsequently, you have the option to make payment using Bitcoin, thus enabling the utilization of your gift cards at establishments that do not accept Bitcoin as a form of payment. This is a preferred method among influential members of the Bitcoin industry to utilize their Bitcoin holdings, enabling them to circumvent the transaction fees typically imposed by Bitcoin wallet administrators.

Buying Offline

There is a limited presence of retailers providing the online option to transact with Bitcoin, and an even scarcer amount of retailers offering the opportunity to make Bitcoin purchases offline.

As of 2017, no dominant retailers possess the capacity to process Bitcoin transactions in physical stores. They would necessitate specialized machinery, which would simply incur excessive expenses if deployed in all locations.

However, certain brick-and-mortar establishments do offer the option for customers to make payments using Bitcoin. Most of these establishments tend to cater to specific, specialized markets.

A viable choice available to retailers is the integration of Bitcoin payment options into their customer offerings by utilizing the Shopify platform. In that location, patrons have the option to utilize the payment procedure (both digitally and physically) and determine their preference in terms of using their Bitcoin wallet for payment.

Bitcoin-Only

There are certain establishments where the only available means of payment is through Bitcoin. These websites and establishments are typically characterized as market-style platforms that explicitly designate themselves as exclusive Bitcoin venues. One can ascertain their presence in any of these locations by virtue of the numerous merchants who utilize these platforms. If you have the desire to acquire Bitcoin, you may also utilize one of these marketplaces to vend your wares – numerous Bitcoin proprietors initiated their journey in this manner.

Please note that in order to access these platforms and their associated marketplaces, it is necessary to possess a wallet identification number, which serves as a prerequisite for verifying the availability of Bitcoin prior to gaining entry to the site.

Huge Purchases

There exists a group of individuals who have acquired residential properties exclusively through the utilization of Bitcoin. Naturally, these individuals possess the means to acquire a residence without resorting to a mortgage, opting instead to employ Bitcoin as a form of payment, comparable to conventional cash transactions for home purchases. A property was acquired through the use of Bitcoin for a sum exceeding one million dollars, making it one of the most expensive houses ever transacted in this manner.

It is quite probable that the buyer or seller of the property in question was among the initial holders of Bitcoin.

The Silk Road

Prior to its cessation and subsequent inquiries in 2015, the Silk Road held the prominent position as the foremost marketplace for conducting transactions utilizing the digital currency known as Bitcoin. A multitude of individuals frequented the platform for regular trading activities, engaging in diverse transactions involving the Bitcoin holdings in their possession.

Individuals who availed themselves of the services provided by the Silk Road were able to procure a wide array of goods, ranging from illicit marijuana to unauthorized reproductions of movies that had not yet been officially released on the DVD format. Certain purchases were straightforward, although they could be considered illicit due to the requirement of governmental regulation. Other individuals, such as victims of human trafficking, were deemed unlawful and morally reprehensible.

Unusual Purchases

One of the most remarkable acquisitions, or opulent, made using Bitcoin was the procurement of a helicopter. Although the specific details regarding the purchase and the identity of the purchaser remain undisclosed, it is purported that the individuals involved in the transaction are reputed acquaintances and have been actively engaged in the Bitcoin market since its inception. It is highly plausible that this entity may have been connected to the home acquisition process, or at the very least, acquainted with one of the individuals involved, as the Bitcoin realm represents a closely-knit community.

Technology Purchases

While this fact may not come as a surprise, particularly in light of the strong association between Bitcoin and technology, it is important to note that a substantial proportion of Bitcoin transactions are conducted for technology-related purposes. These acquisitions encompass a wide range of items, ranging from state-of-the-art electronic devices to innovative methodologies for enhancing technological practices within the community. It is imperative to acknowledge that not all transactions or exchanges involving Bitcoin are necessarily linked to the realm of the Internet and technology. However, it is worth noting that a significant proportion of such transactions and trades do occur within this domain, given that Bitcoin operates exclusively within the online sphere as a concept of currency and trading.

Expanding Bitcoin Investments

Certain individuals have opted to acquire additional Bitcoin with the sole purpose of utilizing it for financial transactions.

Purchasing Bitcoin with the intention of investment is indeed a commendable notion; however, acquiring it solely for the purpose of online or offline transactions may not be the most prudent decision. Given the perpetual volatility of Bitcoin, establishing a precise valuation for commodities transacted in this digital currency proves to be a formidable challenge.

Utilizing your Bitcoin for transactions may result in a financial loss.

The sole means of safeguarding oneself against fraudulent transactions and ensuring a legitimate exchange of goods and services with Bitcoin is by possessing a substantial quantity of the cryptocurrency. Upon reaching a specific threshold, it becomes economically advantageous for individuals to opt for purchasing goods directly using Bitcoin, rather than engaging in the process of selling it and incurring the associated seller's fee.

Dividing the Bitcoin

Due to the availability of numerous affordable items priced below $1,000, a mechanism has been devised to facilitate the division of Bitcoin. Individuals who engage in investment activities may also partake in this opportunity by purchasing fractional amounts of

Bitcoin. This facilitates investment and enables seamless transactions using Bitcoin, thereby ensuring individuals do not face complete loss of their original Bitcoin investment.

Advice And Techniques For Optimizing Ethereum Utilization

Utilizing platforms such as ethereum may prove challenging, and it is plausible that you may encounter frustrations during your experience. However, with the appropriate guidelines and techniques at your disposal, the utilization of the system can be significantly facilitated. As you further utilize the system, your proficiency in navigating such challenges, as previously discussed in a preceding chapter, will enhance expeditiously. Therefore, it is advisable to leverage the advice and guidance offered by experienced Ethereum users in order to circumvent errors and pitfalls they have previously encountered.

Your password

You have been informed of this on numerous occasions, and you will once again receive the same information here. It is imperative to create a strong and highly secure password. It is not common to encounter individuals who employ robust password practices, and by conducting thorough investigation, it is often possible to ascertain their passwords in order to gain unauthorized access to their accounts. Consequently, by employing a strong password, you will effectively safeguard your cryptocurrency holdings, thus minimizing the risk of coin loss.

Consider your password to be a protective barrier for your account. It will effectively deter unauthorized access to your account; hence, the higher the strength of your password, the more robust your security shield will become. Furthermore, it is essential to ensure the utmost security of your crypto assets, necessitating the establishment of a robust password. Similar to the level of security one would require for a bank account, a strong and secure password is imperative.

Should you be unfamiliar with the composition of a robust password, please refer to the following set of instructions.

Letters

Numbers

Symbols

The minimum required length is sixteen characters.

While it is not mandatory for all passwords to comprise sixteen characters, it is noteworthy that the longer the password, the diminished likelihood that unauthorized individuals can successfully breach it and gain access to your cryptocurrency wallet. Long passwords can pose challenges in terms of memorization, hence it is advisable to document them in order to facilitate recall. Additionally, there will be accessible resources online that can assist you in generating passwords that are both easy to remember and highly secure. However, refrain from utilizing a password manager as doing so may grant unauthorized individuals the capability to retrieve the password if they successfully breach your computer, as opposed to making direct attempts to infiltrate your account. Password managers can be highly beneficial when utilized for everyday login requirements. However, as previously mentioned, it is important to be cautious as unauthorized individuals may gain access to all your passwords by successfully infiltrating your computer system. In addition to forfeiting your cryptocurrency holdings, you will also relinquish your identity.

Secure your wallet with encryption.

Cryptocurrency wallets are sophisticated software platforms designed to securely store and manage the information pertaining to your digital currency assets. Each wallet will present varying degrees of security, yet their overarching aim is to furnish users with a robust level of protection. If you find yourself in a time-sensitive situation where you need to swiftly establish a wallet, it is recommended to utilize MyEtherWallet. Being the initial ethereum wallet created, it garners the most trust as a highly efficient and reliable wallet option. However, irrespective of the strength of your wallet password, it remains ineffective in thwarting the efforts of hackers utilizing sophisticated techniques such as keylogging and other advanced attacks to illicitly acquire your information.

Sync your wallet

Considering your wallet as equivalent to your bank account will prove advantageous to you. Funds will be deposited into your wallet, and it is imperative that you prevent unauthorized access to them. Therefore, it would be advisable for you to locate an online software application that offers you the functionality to create a backup of your wallet. It is advisable to ensure the backup of your wallet. Some programs provide the feature of enabling the initial synchronization and subsequently automatically synchronizing whenever there are updates to your account. By performing a wallet backup, you will safeguard your account against potential system malfunctions and crashes. However, it is imperative to not only preserve the backup of your wallet, but also to ensure the backup of your cryptographic keys. Creating a backup of your keys will ensure your capacity to regain access to your wallet. Furthermore, in the event of key loss, it should be noted that external retrieval will not be possible. Hence, it is imperative to have a reliable backup location for your keys. It would be prudent to consider safeguarding your wallet by storing its contents on an external hard drive, transferring them onto a flash drive, or alternatively, printing them out. Additionally, there is the option to transform it into a json file, thereby enabling offline storage.

Here are a few alternative options for backups that you may consider using:

Backup wallet.dat

Bip 32 cryptographic wallet.

Use multi-signatures

The presence of multiple signatures implies that there will be a plurality of individuals associated with your wallet. However, it is not necessary to include another individual on your crypto wallet if you wish to avoid doing so. You may utilize an alternative device that you possess, provided that it is not the principal device associated with your ethereum account. However, should you place your trust in an individual to safeguard your digital currency, you would have the opportunity to enlist the services of a business partner or your spouse. Truly, you may rely upon individuals whom you possess sufficient confidence in, so as to prevent any unauthorized appropriation of your financial resources. The number of signatures necessary to finalize a transaction will be contingent upon the number of signatures established during the initial configuration of your wallet. Several web wallets will provide you with the alternative of employing multiple signatures, aiming to reduce instances of fraud regarding your digital currency.

Certain wallets include:

Blocktrail

Coinbase

Chapter Two

Guide on the Process of Purchasing

Traditionally, we have become accustomed to procuring cryptocurrencies through reputable platforms such as Coinbase, while seated in front of our personal computers. Nevertheless, if you are seeking a mobile application that facilitates the seamless exchange and trading of cryptocurrencies, even when not in proximity of your computer, this chapter will acquaint you with a selection of reputable applications provided by esteemed cryptocurrency exchanges.

1. The company known as Binance

Binance is currently recognized as an exceptionally swiftly expanding platform for cryptocurrency trading within the contemporary marketplace. The exchange provides a comprehensive mobile application that enables users to engage in trading activities while on the move. The Binance mobile application is accessible for download on both Android and iOS devices. Furthermore, Binance provides a desktop application as well. The platform offers support for an array of cryptocurrencies such as bitcoin, ethereum, NEO, IOTA, and various others.

2. "Gate.io, an established platform,

Gate.io is a trustworthy platform that facilitates the trading of numerous cryptocurrencies. The fully operational mobile application also allows users to incorporate fiat currency by means of an AliPay account. On this platform, individuals have the opportunity to engage in the trading of numerous digital currencies such as bitcoin, ethereum, Tether, and QTUM, offering the flexibility to exchange them for any other preferred cryptocurrency.

3. The establishment known as Bibox

Bibox is a mobile application that facilitates intelligent and secure trading. The platform provides multiple functionalities, including a comprehensive charting package that will foster an appreciation for advanced technological capabilities.

4. Bitfinex is a cryptocurrency exchange platform.

Bitfinex, recognized as one of the leading cryptocurrency platforms, provides a mobile application that facilitates seamless cryptocurrency trading and enables users to conveniently deposit funds to their Bitfinex accounts while remaining mobile. Bitfinex is known for facilitating the trading of highly sought-after digital assets such as Bitcoin, Ripple, IOTA, Ethereum, Monero, OMG, NEO, QTUM, ZEC, and DASH.

5. KuCoin is a reputable cryptocurrency exchange platform.

KuCoin is a recently-established cryptocurrency platform that provides a dependable mobile application, facilitating seamless cryptocurrency trading for users. Furthermore, aside from featuring numerous widely-used digital currencies, KuCoin also provides the opportunity to acquire GAS through the retention of NEO tokens.

Commencement of Token Sales

An Initial Coin Offering (ICO) is a financial mechanism that facilitates the acquisition of funds by investors through the utilization of digital currencies such as bitcoin or Ethereum. To clarify, an Initial Coin Offering (ICO) is a form of crowdsourcing wherein a fledgling company offers a newly created digital currency to the general public for sale. ICOs bear resemblance to Initial Public Offerings, as they offer companies the opportunity to raise capital for projects by means of issuing digital tokens.

Within the context of initial coin offerings (ICOs), cryptocurrency companies engage in the practice of preselling their respective cryptocurrencies or tokens. The funds collected during the event are subsequently utilized by companies as supplementary financing for the advancement of an application, software, or the cryptocurrency itself.

The majority of startups tend to favor initial coin offerings (ICOs) due to their ability to swiftly obtain funding from a global audience without geographical constraints. Moreover, this approach allows them to maintain managerial authority over the organization as they are not diluting ownership by involving external investors; instead, they are offering a prospective service for sale.

"An Initial Coin Offering typically encompasses the subsequent components:

• A website encompassing comprehensive details concerning the project, including its objectives, the profile of the individuals involved in its pursuit, and information on the token structure throughout the various fundraising stages of the Initial Coin Offering (ICO), comprising both the PRE-ICO and ICO stages. Additionally, it would be beneficial to include pertinent details pertaining to the allocated discounts extended to early investors.

• A comprehensive written report elucidating the intricacies of the business model. Typically, this document spans from 20 to 25 pages in length.

Investing in Initial Coin Offering (ICO) tokens can confer advantages to investors as outlined in the smart contract, providing potential benefits in the future. Moreover, the value of the tokens has the potential to appreciate rapidly, enabling profitable transactions through timely buying and selling.

However, it must be noted that the ICO also presents some unfavorable aspects. With the prevalence of numerous Initial Coin Offerings occurring on a continual basis, and the overarching reality being that a substantial proportion of newly introduced digital currencies typically fail to attain significant progress. Certain initial coin offerings (ICOs) even go so far as to be fraudulent or demonstrate characteristics of pyramid schemes, with promoters inflating the value of essentially valueless tokens in an attempt to make sales.

If one desires to engage in an initial coin offering (ICO), it is highly advisable to conduct thorough research in order to ascertain the nature of the purchase being made.

"Primarily, it is imperative that you refrain from participating in an Initial Coin Offering (ICO) in the following circumstances:

• The individuals responsible for it remain anonymous: While the principles of decentralization and anonymity are highly esteemed in the realm of cryptocurrency, entrusting one's funds to an unknown party should be deemed unacceptable. If you lack knowledge regarding the identities of the founders, it is likely ill-advised to consider investing in such a venture.

• The offer appears excessively advantageous: If it becomes evident that the revenue percentage significantly exceeds the average and lacks a reasonable justification, it is highly likely that investing in this ICO would not be advisable.

• It is devoid of a definitive plan or strategic direction. Any reputable startup will engage in the development of a comprehensive strategic plan that provides insight into the future trajectory of the currency. If a definitive trajectory for the cryptocurrency's future is not discernible, it would be prudent to reconsider your investment decision.

How ICOs Work?

Like any endeavor, the inception of all Initial Coin Offerings (ICOs) arises from an initial concept. Through the utilization of Initial Coin Offerings (ICOs), a nascent company formulates a conceptualization for a blockchain-driven undertaking and presents it to the collective assemblage.

If the concept garners support from community members, the startup proceeds to diligently develop a comprehensive whitepaper encompassing intricate particulars of the project. This generally encompasses details pertaining to the technical aspects of the project, its plans, and the personnel associated with the project.

Numerous additional details are subsequently determined, encompassing the allocation quantity of tokens, individual token pricing, as well as the manner in which tokens will be utilized within the project's ecosystem.

After the identification of these aspects, marketing initiatives are subsequently initiated to stimulate progress, and a date for the initial coin offering (ICO) is disclosed to commence the token sale. Typically, a specified time frame is allotted during which the collection of funds will take place. The sale concludes upon the successful acquisition of the necessary funds.

Following the closure of sales, investors will subsequently commence receiving their tokens, and arrangements will be implemented for their deployment on exchange platforms to facilitate trading.

www.ingramcontent.com/pod-product-compliance
Lightning Source LLC
Chambersburg PA
CBHW071700210326
41597CB00017B/2261